# VIDEO GAME

# ADDICTION

# VIDEO GAME ADDICTION

*Writers:*

Austin Mardon

Catherine Mardon

Monica Thakadu

Botho Modutlwe

Kirithika Bharatselvam

Hailey Borys

Maya Nagorski

Brianna Bedran

*Editor/APM:*

Anastasiya Yermolenko

**GM**
★
**PRESS**

First Printing: 2021


Cover Design and typeset by Clare Dalton


ISBN 978-1-77369-641-6

E-book ISBN 978-1-77369-642-3


Golden Meteorite Press

103 11919 82 St NW

Edmonton, AB T5B 2W3

www.goldenmeteoritepress.com

# CONTENTS

# CHAPTER 1:
# HISTORY OF VIDEO GAMES

BY MONICA THAKADU

History is something that we should take into consideration when talking about all those things that matter the most to us. We need to know most importantly the dates, causes or mission of an act or event or concept. The same thing applies to video games; we need to take note of its whereabouts, why, when and who invented them. Henceforth this chapter is going to look at the history of video games in more detail.

Video games came far more than we could ever think or imagine. They began as early as the 1950s and 1960s by computer scientists in research labs. However, the main question still stands - "who invented video games?" Therefore, there is no 'how we are going to discuss about the history of video games' without making mention of Ralph H. Baer, Steve Russell and William Higginbotham (though we won't be able to cover Steve Russell).

# THE INVENTION OF VIDEO GAMES

## (i) WILLIAM HIGGINBOTHAM

The invention of video games evolved around a physicist by the name of William Higginbotham (October 25, 1910 – November 1994). It was in October 1958 when William Higginbotham took the first step in history and invented the first video game Pong at a Brookhaven National Laboratory Open House. Higginbotham believed that many people had the misconception regarding the purpose of science and inventing the first video game. More especially in the science laboratory will definitely show people that science is not all about war and destruction (A brief history of video games).

Higginbotham made some drawings and blueprints for the game. Its circuit was bodily built with resistors, capacitors, relay as well as transistors. Due to the fact that the video game was made in the science lab, it was therefore only visible or accessible as well as highly valued and appreciated by the visitors of the laboratory. He called the game "Tennis for two". As it usually seems like it is very difficult for scientists to be well known for their inventions, William Higginbotham experienced the same thing. He was more popular as an inventor of video games in 1982 after an article in Creative Computing Magazine, (History of video games-Wikipedia).

As years passed by, a cheese company owner, Nolan Bushnell together with Ted Dabney formed a company called Atari in 1972. Atari then discovered an improved version of Pong the same year it was formed. But before then Nutting Associates introduced the first sold out arcade video game console known as Computer space in 1971.Then sooner after Pong was introduced in 1972, this gave rise to the Magnavox Odyssey formed and released by Magnavox. Paper money, cards and dice characterized it and it was the first home video game console.

Let us just make a list of the 10 oldest video games consoles down for you to be able to understand deeply. Note that though some sources say that the first video game was invented in 1940 whilst we mentioned earlier that video games began in the 1950s and 1960s; video games were mostly released around the early 1970s (10 oldest video games in the world/oldest.org).

**Ten oldest video games in the world**

- Computer Space = Released in 1971

- Pong = Released in November 29, 1972

- Magnavox Odyssey = Released in September 1972 (NB: SOME SOURCES SAY AUGUST 1972)

- Space Race = Released in July 16, 1973

- Doom = Released in December 10, 1973

- Gran Tank 10 = Released in May 1974

- Entertainment Software Ratings Board = Released in September 1974

- Gun Fight (OR Western Gun)= Released in 1975

- Game Boy = Release in April 21, 1989


NB: Because of emergence of so many video game consoles into the entertainment industry, there was market congestion and competition. In 1983, Atari and Midway (The Company that changed the game console "Pack Man into Puc Man" competed for customers). This was an era called "Atari Shock in Japan". Gaming met the real world in 11988.

The different game consoles of that time are:

# Color Game Series by  Japanese Company (1977)

# Puc Man (1980)

# Ultimo (1980)

# Commodore 64 home computer (1982)

# Mario Bros (1983)


Later on

# Tetris (1984)

# Nintendo Entertainment System (NES) console (1985)

# SimCity (1989)

Now that we have talked about William Higginbotham and his impact in the entertainment industry let us now talk about Ralph H. Baer.

## (ii) RALPH H. BAER

Ralph H. Baer is an inventor who is genuinely regarded as "The father of Video Games ". He invented several video games more than any other inventor in this field did though he is popularly known as the inventor of Simon Electronic Game; (The father of Video Games: Ralph H. Baer Prototypes and Electronic Games). He also developed a device that worked well with the television monitor. Here are his video game inventions:

• Brown Box Golf Game Accessory, 1968

• Magnavox Odyssey, 1972

• Simon Electronic Game , 1978

• Maniac Electronic Game , 1979

NB: Computer games in 1966 and bell labs helped in developing computer game programs in 1971 and 1973. There was also advancement in technology between the late 1990s and the early 2000s. Many different game consoles like Monkey (1990), Wolfenstein 3D ( 1992), Play station By Sony (1994), Command and Conquer (1995), Tomb Raider ( 1996), Age of Empires (1997), Sims (2000), Online World of Warcraft ( 2004), Grand Theft Auto: San Andrea's (2004), Super Mario Galaxy (2007), Minecraft (2010) and Red Redemption 2 (2019). The 3D graphic platforms, CD-ROMS and Graphic cards began to emerge .Due to high usage of internet it was now easier to introduce and access video games via online. Microsoft X Box line, hardware and software services also innovated the efficiency of their use. Different game genres such as Racing, target shooting , hide and seek , and star trek also emerged; ( First Generation of Video Game Consoles-Wikipedia).

So, which console has the largest life span?

- Farnicorn ( 10 years, 347 days)

- PC Engine with CD- ROM (10 years , 183 days)

- Super Farnicorn ( 10 years, 11 days)

- XBox 360 ( 9 years, 345 days)

- Playstation 1 ( 9 years , 164 days )

- Wii ( 8 years, 151 days )

- Dreamcast ( 8 years, 103 days )

To sum up we could say that Farnicorn is typically the oldest video game console OR the video game console with the largest life span. We could also add by saying that the Electronic Entertainment Expo (E3) was the world's biggest event in history. Bertie "The Brain "(1950) of Tic- Tac-Toe by Josef Kates became the first video game to be shown in public. We could also add by saying that Space Invaders was the first arcade video game to record and display high scores.

Many people have fallen in love with soccer as the main video game in Play Station in recent years. Passing by, Soccer originates from China using different names in history up until England changed its name to what we now call football just like the British. China is therefore the world's largest gaming industry or revenue. Statistics show that many people play video games during leisure time for fun regardless of gender or age. Let us say a big Thank You to Sony.

## CONCLUSION

We now know that:

- Video games began in the early 1950s and 1960s by Computer Scientists in Science labs.

- William Higginbotham made a gateway to the invention of video games in 1958 that developed into what we now see today as game genres and consoles together with other contributors, (what was the first video game? – Plarium).

- Ralph H. Baer is the "Father of video games ". He invented several different video games like Brown Box Golf Game Accessory in 1968, Magnavox Odyssey in 1972, Simon Electronic Game in 1978 and Maniac Electronic Game in 1979, (American History).

- Computer systems in 1966 and Bell Labs helped to develop computer game programs in 1971 and 1973. Mainframe computers are also introduced (A brief history of video games).

- Video game is introduced in television because of Ralph H. Baer's innovation in 1967.

- Computer Space became the first commercial arcade video game introduced by the Nutting Associates in 1971.

- Nolan Bushnell and Ted Dabney formed Atari in 1972.

- Atari introduced Magnavox Odyssey by Magnavox and Ralph H. Baer and Pong in 1972.

- Atari's video computer system is also formed in 1977.

- William Higginbotham became popular as an inventor in 1982 after an Article in Creative Computing Magazine.

- The two companies Atari and Midway compete. There was the "Atari shock "in 1983 due to market congestion and competition from Midway and other people.

- Gaming meets the real world in 1988.

- Sony introduces Play station and the internet is also introduced.

- In the late 1990s and the early 2000s the internet is introduced

- Into the world.

- There is emergence of so many different types of video games, game consoles and genres as years goes by as well as advancements in technology. CD – ROMS, Graphic cards, Microsoft XBox line, Wii and Nintendo switch.

- A larger internet coverage leads to improved release of video games online leading to an easy access worldwide.

- Hardware and software services also led to their innovation.

- People today play video games be it on mobile phones or personal computers online. Some of the video games are even available offline.

- The main played video game of recent times is Football and the video game genre is the Red Redemption 2 of 2019 in Youtube.

# CHAPTER 2:

# WHY DO PEOPLE LOVE VIDEO GAMES? THE BACKGROUND PSYCHOLOGY

**BOTHO MODUTLWE**

The love for video games has long started with the invention of technology, which brought along the obsession for playing them. As everyone has different reasons for doing different activities or even the same activity, it is the same with playing video games. People all over the world have several reasons for playing video games. As the intention of inventing it was with the intention of some sort of entertainment, video gaming has not only become something that people want to and love to play but it has also become a career. People earn a living and survive out of just sitting at their comfortable homes and competing with others from across the world, just like people who play physically in the field with similar rules and regulations. In this context, this patent is to specify the real reasons behind the love for video gaming and add on the psychological background for it.

Video games are known to teach different skills as well as hinder others. In this regard, we are to know that video gaming can be vital for teaching good visual attention skills and paying attention especially to children. This is because players are required to monitor a field of view that is crowded with distractors to quickly locate targets when they suddenly appear. They should be able to make rapid shifts with focus switching their attention from one urgent task to the next. These skills are related to what psychologists call 'attention switching' or 'task switching.'(Parenting Science 2021). On the other hand, video gaming may have effects on the other type of attention that is careful and sustained, however one may develop what is called reactive control.

A big reason why people play video games so much is because they use them as an escape from the problems, stresses, worries and anxieties of the world. A speech by a gamer said, "Sometimes it's nice to put on the shoes of a made-up character and forget about all our troubles. I know that after I have had a hard day, I come and put on a headset and play a good game." He continued to say that action movies are his favorite as they are sucked into the game's world and forgets about everything around them. On the other hand, violent games, even though criticized by the whole world, especially parents of their kids, they are good for getting rid of anger in a much healthier way. In his words, Bob Dylan says the people who bottle up their anger and do not get it out are the ones who end up with problems. Dylan said that the average person that play violent games are not violent, putting himself as a typical example that he has never been involved in any physical fight in his whole life even though he loves playing fighting and shooting games. (GamesBeat 2013).

Games such as video puzzles, computer chess, are also known to relieve the mind from the daily exhaustions. One can just download the applications into their device and play alone, compete with the computer or with someone else. Mostly, these are games that people download in their devices either a phone, a tablet or computer and mostly can be played when one is offline. For some people playing video games is used as a way to get connection with people from different parts of the world through streaming games such as PUGB. They get to make new friends from across continents and get to learn their kind of lifestyles. In these times of coronavirus pandemic, that has affected the whole world, there should be a high record of many new gamers who were introduced to the gaming world, as people had to stay indoors for a very long time without contact with their friends. The online platforms were the only things available for them to socialize and play together. This may have triggered more love for video gaming when people and states were on lockdown. Amongst all, there is the largest well-known and most used excuse from the people who play video games when they were asked to give the real reason why they love video games, which is entertainment. A lot of people will say they play video games to have fun and to try to get around boredom and to make some difference to their boring and monotonous lifestyles.

Three invincible needs have been identified to describe the reason why people play video games (teach thought n.d.) amongst them Scott Rigby says Immersyve's complex needs-satisfaction metrics narrow down to three basic categories. First, which is the 'need for competence,' he says people like to feel successful, and we like to feel like we're growing and progressing in our knowledge and accomplishments, hence video games give us the feeling of accomplishment and fulfill our desire to feel competent. Rigby's second psychological need is 'autonomy,' "people dislike being manipulated, hence imprisonment is a punishment, and why we feel an innate urge to rebel against slavery." Therefore, gamers use video games to give themselves that autonomy and feel that freedom and like they have escaped from all their manipulative environments. His final human need is the 'relatedness,' gamers are able to fulfill the feeling of mattering to others through playing online even when playing with people who are not real. This is a much better way to help people who are lonely; whom feel like everyone and no one reject them really cares about them. Moving on, Kayla Matthews's 10 Reasons Why People Who Play Video Games Are Happier, says they are more connected to their inner child. Gaming adults have a chance to engage in playful behavior, the same way we used to play when we were young which helps to enjoy life and live happily. Adults are also exposed to greater creativity and imagination, whether it is a realistic, a Call of Duty or a highly imaginative video game; just using your imagination to put yourself in their world is a highly stimulating exercise for the brain, (Lifehack, 2021). "My research on teen's technology use shows that teen boys use this space as a new way of hanging out with each other." Said by Joanne Orlando, he continued to say that the social connection that men find in playing video games is far more important to them than being in an actual game. The talk and sense of comradery that comes with being with those of your gender is more valuable to them, (The Sydney Morning Herald, 2018).

A number of video gamers are known to be anti-social because they are used to connecting with people through a screen and playing video games hence they are not good at socializing with people at a psychosocial level. When they get to the outside world, they experience a completely new environment, which makes it becomes hard to familiarize themselves with the right behavioral aspects of the society. Addicted video gamers have been identified to have personality traits such as low self-esteem, low self-efficacy, anxiety disorders, aggression and depression. However, it still remains unclear as to what extent people's various reasons for playing video games are differentially related to their psychological functioning (Frontiers in Psychology, 2019). Scientists have been unable to identify the real causal link between playing video games and the acts of violence in the real world. Video gaming however has shown to have impacts in some parts of the brain, the way it performs and its structure. From the research made and studies undertaken it has been proven that video gaming affects attention such as sustained and selective attention. Playing video games also affects the size and competence of parts of the brain responsible for identifying the relationship between visual and spatial abilities where their hippocampus was enlarged. Structural alterations in the neural reward system have been identified amongst gaming addicts, evidence of cravings have been detected in parts of their brains, (MedicalNewsToday, 2017). Addiction in gaming leads to the release of high quantities of dopamine in the brain, which stimulates receptors that in turn drive the impulse to repeat the behavior in question. This behavior gets to a point where now the addiction has developed into tolerance until now the brain chemistry normalizes it as a habit, (UK REHAB, n.d.)

The beginning of the love for video gaming eventually leads to addiction to it. Failure to control the amount of time one spends on playing video games is hence really dangerous. The danger of video gaming is still an ongoing research considering how much damage it entails in an individual's brain and behavior. Even though the love for video games is seemingly increasing day by day, scientists are also working to identify as many pros and cons of the habit of video gaming. In these times of Coronavirus pandemic people are encouraged to find all the available sources to maintain the maximum isolation to avoid the spread of the virus. This has encouraged a lot of people to prefer playing online than having physical contact.

# CHAPTER 3:

# WHAT ARE THE PROS AND CONS OF GAMING?

## KIRITHIKA BHARATSELVAM

From Pokémon to Call of Duty to Cooking Mama, video games can range from thousands of different genres catering to almost anyone regardless of age, gender, or area of interest. Despite the variation, video games usually carry a harsh stigma from grown adults, parents and the media while they have become increasingly popular amongst kids and teens. However, are the harsh criticisms of video games exaggerated? Is it true that video games have harmful effects that translate into the real world? In what ways can they be beneficial? This chapter will discuss both the pros and cons of video gaming in the context of educational use, improving health, and skill enhancement. On the other hand, discussing why it can decrease academics, increase the sexualisation of women, and increase aggressive and violent behaviours.

## CON: DECREASED ACADEMIC PERFORMANCE

With adolescents playing video games for 7 hours a week, where males play for an average of 13 hours per week while females play for an average of five hours (Gentile et al., 2004), gaming has become a prime activity for children to partake in. However, there is a direct correlation between the amount of time students play video games and their academic performance. For instance, high school students scored lower marks and lower overall grades in English classes when reported to be spending money on video games or spending more time playing them. Similar results have also been shown amongst college students as academic performance decreased due to the amount of time that video games are played for (Gentile et al., 2004). According to a study on 607 8th to 9th-grade students, female students scored slightly higher averages than their male counterparts did. The female students were reported to enjoy playing violent video games less than their male counterparts did and for less time per week (Gentile et al., 2004). Therefore, showing a negative correlation between student academics and the amount of time video games are played for. Additionally, the time spent playing video games replaces the amount of time that children can engage in social or educational activities such as playing outside with friends, reading books, studying/doing homework, or spending quality time with family (Gentile et al., 2004).

Video games can also cause attention deficiency in children when exposed to video games in their childhood, potentially lasting into their late adolescence and into early adulthood (Swing et al., 2010). Poorer grades can also be a result of poor sleep quality. According to a study, seventeen males between the ages of 15-17, played action-packed and violent video games for 150 minutes leading to sleep efficiency decreasing by 7% compared to playing video games for 50 minutes. This had reduced sleep efficiency by below 85%, the clinically accepted cut-off that would indicate sleep disorders. However, playing video games for 50 minutes was within a normal range (King et al., 2013). Video gaming can impact sleep quality in multiple ways, such as less time spent sleeping, circadian rhythm delay due to screen brightness, increased physiological arousal, and increased levels of tiredness (Cain & Gradisar, 2010). This could affect a child's ability to focus on tedious school tasks and can consequently decrease their performance on school-related work, possibly reducing academic performance.

## CONS: INCREASED AGGRESSION AND VIOLENCE

Though video games expand to many genres, up to 89% of them, the majority, include violence, half of the games containing serious violence against other characters within the game. Thus, the majority of video games being consumed and purchased contain various acts of violence. Playing these types of video games has been shown to affect people regardless of age or gender. Effects include decreased prosocial behaviours, increased physiological arousal, and increased aggressive cognition, behaviour, and emotions (Gentile et al., 2004). Studies have found that there is a correlation between aggressiveness and exposure to violent video games. Research conducted on violence in movies and television in 30+ years proposes that engaging in violent video gaming in the long-term can negatively affect development (Anderson & Murphy, 2003). A study on eighth to ninth-grade students showed a significant correlation between playing violent video games and demonstrating aggressiveness (Gentile et al., 2004). Non-violent video games were favoured amongst 50% of girls, while only 30% of the boys favoured games with no violence. Boys also preferred more violent video games compared to girls. And when asked to rate the amount of violence they enjoyed on a scale of 1 (non-violent) to 10 (extremely violent), 68% of boys rated their preference 6-10 points while only 22% of girls preferred this amount of violence (Gentile et al., 2004). In total, in the past year, 34% of students reported getting into a physical fight/altercation, and 23% argued with their teacher almost daily or weekly. Breaking this statistic down, boys were found to be more aggressive than girls as 28% of them got into arguments with their teachers' weekly/daily while only 17% of girls reported this. In addition, physical fights were reported by 47% of boys, whereas 19% of the girls reported this within the past year (Gentile et al., 2004). Altogether, when adolescents engage with violent video games for prolonged periods of time, it can increase violent and aggressive behaviours amongst youth.

## CONS: SEXUALISATION AND OBJECTIFICATION OF WOMEN

Overall, video games tend to create a hostile atmosphere for women as video game content consists of negative perspectives on women as a result of extreme sexualisation, dehumanization, sexism, and objectification (Burnay, n.d.). This is seen not only within video games but also within the industry and the broader community. Online gaming has created an environment where male video game players can spread their negative views on women to others in the video game community. Data collected from 294 gamers show that female gamers experienced hostile and sexist behaviours such as discrimination, verbal contempt, and sexual harassment from male players. These negative attitudes may be a result of male and female video game characters being represented through stereotypes both physically in addition to their purpose/role within the game. For example, men who played a sexual female character reported less positive attitudes towards the physical capabilities of women compared to the participants who were female (Burnay, n.d.). Either a study conducted on adolescents between the ages of 12 and 15 played The Story of Arado with a male character that was not sexualized or with a female character that was. After playing, it was found that their tolerance concerning sexual harassment and rape myth acceptance significantly rose (Burnay, n.d.). All in all, this could have detrimental effects on females in the real world as males inherit sexist thinking from playing video games with sexual female characters.

## PRO: IMPROVES SCHOOL ENVIRONMENT AND ACADEMIC PERFORMANCE

In school, educational games are significantly utilized to teach various subjects, skills, and materials that can also be accessed at home for further development and learning (Weigle, 2017). Video games' interactive and entrancing nature makes them excellent teaching tools that can enhance students' learning. Video games have endless possibilities on what they can teach, and numerous educational games for an extensive range of students have already been created. For example, Immune Attack, a video game that teaches different infections and immune cells. Players must try to identify the infection and then train the character's immune system against it using a variety of objects in order to stop the invasion of pathogens. Another example is Quest Atlantis that aims to teach inquiry and research skills by providing players multiple 3D virtual environments where kids from ages 9 to 12 can interview virtual communities, research, and conduct studies. In addition, Discover Babylon is a multiplayer video game that involves the use of accurate scientific and historical information to answer educational questions based on the 3D simulation. This game is aimed towards 8-14-year-olds to understand Mesopotamia as a whole, including facts about their trade, businesses, and the overall society (Annetta, 2008).

Students can also improve their academics and absorb information better by using video gaming as an outlet to reduce stress, reward academic achievement, gain technical words video games use for further understanding in the classroom, and create more friends through online gaming (Adžić et al., 2021). Video games can also improve learning for those on the autism spectrum, as video games can help accommodate for their condition by teaching skills that autistic individuals need, like learning to identify the alphabet to eventually memorize it (Selvakumarasamy et al., 2021). A systematic review from 16 studies including 575 participants showed that video games have the potential to be included as training surgical skills. Of the 16 included studies, surgical skills in robotic surgery and laparoscopy were frequently tested. The study concluded that there is a positive correlation between the usage of training with video games and improving the skill-set involved with laparoscopy and robotic surgery (Gupta et al., 2021).

## PRO: IMPROVING MENTAL AND PHYSICAL HEALTH

Video games when played unsupervised or excessively over a prolonged period, can result in numerous negative issues. However, video games have also been shown to influence both mental and physical health positively. In terms of physical health, multiple popular video games can improve hand motor skills, visual attention, contrast sensitivity, strategic and spatial navigation skills (Weigle, 2017). As video games have virtually no limit in their possibilities, they can be created to make things like healthy living into fun tasks that increase motivation and engagement among the public (Weigle, 2017). For instance, video games like Wii Fit and the Just Dance series can be used for exercise. Video games have also been created as treatments for mental health disorders like anxiety and depression and improving behavioural issues. This has been proven to be effective and may be able to also help with schizophrenia (Weigle, 2017). Specialized video games for medical treatments have also been proven to be effective in physical therapy, treatment for obesity and amblyopia and can even be used during medical procedures to divert patients' attention from pain (Weigle, 2017).

## PRO: PERSONAL DEVELOPMENT

In addition to video games being used in education and learning, it can also be used to improve youth development in non-scholarly contexts. Video games can be used for specific tasks to teach youth social, cognitive, and behavioural skills (Weigle, 2017). Furthermore, research has shown that video games increase decision-making skills and are more effective than watching videos (Reynaldo et al., 2021). Video games' effect on behaviour has demonstrated that people may become more disciplined through gaming sessions as video game players are instructed to do certain tasks in a specific way. Usually, a reward and punishment system is enforced where breaking rules can result in a punishment, thus pushing players to abide by the rules (Reynaldo et al., 2021). Cognition skills have also been seen to improve as video games train the human mind through actions and puzzles requiring problem-solving and thinking skills, forcing one to think critically instead of mindlessly going through the game (Reynaldo et al., 2021). Another skill that has been shown to improve during video gaming is time management. Majority of games consist of timed events that must occur, or else one cannot properly "win" the game. Strategy games and other similar genres force video game players to quickly think of how they can split their time into completing various tasks, scenarios, and cases (Reynaldo et al., 2021). Teamwork skills (Adžić et al., 2021) can be obtained through multiplayer games like Fire Boy and Water Girl. In this video game, in each level, the two players must collaborate in order for the levels to be completed and done successfully.

Ultimately, the debate on the good/bad of video games still persists, this chapter detailing the pros and cons of both sides. Pros such as the possibility of improving education for students, personal skills, and both mental and physical health. Moreover, cons such as the possibility of increased violence and aggression, objectification of women, and how it can impair academic performance. Overall, video gaming has both positive and negative effects. However, it is clear that video games should be played in moderation and should be monitored by adult figures in order to minimize the cons detailed in this article and can be subsequently used to improve one's quality of life like through the pros listed.

# CHAPTER 4:

# CAN YOU MAKE MONEY OUT OF PLAYING GAMES ONLINE?

**HAILEY BORYS**

With the introduction of modern amenities such as the internet and personal computers, there was a population shift from the "dark ages" to a society interconnected via technological advancements. All aspects of life were impacted by this transition; one vector took advantage of this transition and grew immensely in video games. During the mid-1970s to early 1980s, video games became common household items; video games themselves began to transition from a pastime hobby to an additional avenue for people looking to make some extra money. With an increase in accessibility, online gaming has led to a steep increase in gambling addictions across the country (Gainsbury, 2015). The introduction of Esports has opened the market to millions who may have never had the opportunity to play or gamble. The popularity of Esports has created symbiotic businesses such as Twitch and YouTube that have created platforms for both streamers to build careers as well as a new venue for customers to watch. Following in the footsteps of Esports is the introduction of online poker and many provincial governments in Canada, including Alberta, have adopted casino websites, beginning mostly as private websites, the field of online casinos. A major hindrance to online gambling sites is accessibility; one way companies get around this is by making mobile applications that can be downloaded via a smartphone rather than websites that are tied to a computer. The introduction of cellphone gambling apps such as Swagbucks and Solitaire provides the ability to gain access to a source of gambling be in the hands of nearly every single adult. Following the invention of the Internet, the world experienced a generational transition to a truly technologically advanced world that witnessed the video gaming market prominently, efficiently, and profitably stake its claim.

Electronic sports (esports) are defined as "a form of sports where the primary aspects of the sport are facilitated by electronic systems; the input of players and teams, as well as the output of the esports system, are mediated by human-computer interfaces" (Hamari & Sjöblom, 2017). This definition does create controversy in the sports community because of the lack of physical exertion during the game, however, these esports can be classed as a sport because it "includes play, the events are organized and governed by rules, includes competition with the outcome of a winner and a loser, and comprises skill" (Bányai et al., 2019). To better understand the abilities of these online players it is important to look into how the players view the sport and more importantly - how they train. A set of esport players were interviewed to gain an understanding of the mental skills and techniques deemed essential to success in the sport, the results included background knowledge of the game, quick and calculated strategies, motivated to continue, having the ability to separate reality from virtual and finally, remain positive and finally warm-up before playing (Himmelstein et al., 2017). Like sports, players compete on teams, often using headsets as a means of virtual communication, spending dedicated time practicing with teammates and hosting fans in arenas and online thus, in turn, and creating a culture for gamers.

Similar to physical sports, there is potential for monetary gains in the field of esport. It is estimated that a majority of revenue, approximately 60-90%, is generated through sponsorships and advertising (Mangeloja, 2019). An example can be seen in Cloud9, a famous esports team that is sponsored by many companies including but not limited to AT&T, BMW, Microsoft and Red Bull (Partners, 2021). The final numbers in esports business models are made up of media rights (20%) and royalties, merchandising and ticket sales make up the final 10-15% (Mangeloja, 2019). In 2015 alone, the rise of esport spectators rose to nearly a hundred million, which allowed for a total sum of sixty-five million dollars US to be given in prize money, further legitimizing the sport (Kresse, 2016; Taylor, 2016). Another source of income is in the form of tournament prizes although this is not a reliable revenue source due to the uncertainty of winning, for this reason, there are only a few games that can sustain themselves professionally, earning the title of superstars (Ward and Harmon, 2019). Global revenue is estimated to reach $1.1 billion in 2020, reflecting an increase of 15.7% from the previous year making the prospect of a career gamer a possibility (Marinkovic, 2020).

Now that esports have been defined and the general economics have been discussed it is crucial to look at the viability of considering a career as a professional gamer. Considering an average for monthly (m) and annual (y) salaries the team makes $4,000/m or $48,000/y; tournament prizes average $8,300/y and from streaming approximately $1,500/m and by using these numbers the average player would potentially make $74,300 per year (Marinkovic, 2020). There are many outlier cases where individuals have made more than the previously mentioned amounts. Looking at the practical economics from the perspective of professional gamers, the top earner of 2017 was Kuro Takhasomi (gamer name KuroKy) who made US$2.44 million (Ward and Harmon, 2019). Looking at this number alone, the earning rate is skewed and suggests that the market is tailored to individuals with superstar talents (Rosen, 1981).

The reality of becoming a professional esports player is very low but that is not to take away from the more realistic ability to make a small earning off streaming online gameplay. Although it is a second-party means to earn money, streaming is nonetheless revenue acquired as a result of online gaming. Today most videogames can be watched through platforms such as YouTube or Twitch, allowing the individual to convert a hobby into more of a dependable revenue source. Due to the nature of subscriber or viewer-based revenue, gamers then need to alter their content in order to retain and gain subscribers, whether that is reflected in the time spent streaming or by the content that is being broadcasted. Twitch, a platform that is based on a monthly subscription provides a generous 50% of its earnings with its streamers (Twitch Affiliate Partner Program, n.d.). To provide an example of better understanding of the pay scale, in Canada, the monthly subscription is $8.99 per month, if a streamer gains fifty followers in one month their payout would result in roughly $225 (Twitch Turbo, n.d.). Similarly, YouTube is another platform that supports gamers in the means of monetary payout based on a variety of factors once the channel has been accepted as a YouTube Partner Program (YPP) within the platform (How to earn money on YouTube, 2021). Using advertising and views as the example, excluding subscribers, the average pay is $0.18 per advertisement view therefore a video with 1000 views would generate roughly $18 per 1000 advertisement views or $3-$5 per 1000 video views (Geyser, 2021). This loss in revenue is calculated by the amount of people who leave the video before watching the advertisements, meaning that in order to secure revenue, the content creator must have a significant influence in the online community.

Esports are only a portion of available options for online games with the ability to produce a payout, moving away from esports; online poker tournaments are commonly associated with payouts and in turn gambling addiction. There are several variables to keep in mind while assessing the viability of an online poker website. From a survey conducted in Stockholm of twenty-four online poker players, it was determined that such players consider the website reputation, the time it takes to receive payouts, website design and reliability and finally the customer service communication and effectiveness (Wood & Griffiths, 2008). For this reason, online poker is appealing to players of all skill levels; beginning players enjoy the convenience, ease of learning and low stakes while the professional players use such platforms to win money while playing several tables at once (Wood & Griffiths, 2008). The factors for increased use of these gambling sites could stem from an increased number of celebrity endorsements and participation in poker playing, advertisements via television and internet, encouraged learning to play for free, low stakes games (as little as one cent) and finally allowing twenty-four-hour access (Griffiths et al., 2006; Wood et al., 2007). From a financial perspective, online poker is enticing as there are "no casino house edge or bookmakers' mark-up on odds" meaning that the earnings made can be attributed to the skill of the individual player rather than predetermined odds (Griffiths, 2005; Griffiths et al., 2006).

Looking at a recent example of online poker, the sizable and enticing payouts can be observed in their entirety. GGPoker, an online European poker platform, hosted the Battle of Malta tournament from July 11 to July 25, 2021 (Shillibier, 2021) In its second year of hosting (2021), Director of Sponsorships & Live Events, John Scanlon claimed there was "at least $25,000,000 in cash to be won...with exclusive trophies, rings and a Player of the Series leaderboard" (Shillibier, 2021). During this event, there were three flagship events including "Siege of Malta" with a €105 buy-in and one million dollar prize pool, "Million$ European Cup" with a €50 buy-in and one million dollar prize pool and finally, the "Main Event" with a €550 buy-in and three million dollar prize pool (Europe's Largest Mid-Stakes Series has Returned, 2021). Focussing on the "Main Event" that took place July 25, 2021, there was recorded 6,591 players who bought into the event raising the anticipated prize pool from €3 million to €3.4 million (Pitt & Glatzer, 2021). The final table had nine participants each of whom won no less than €37,828; in ninth place, NetWizards from Hong Kong walked away with the minimum amount, in comparison Raggaz who won the table claimed a prize of €378,285 (Pitt & Glatzer, 2021). In this account, the prizes were high, an aspect that is enticing to more of a professional player.

So far, both esports and online poker have been discussed; however, there are also regulated means of online gambling where online gameplay can result in a payout. Alberta Gaming, Liquor and Cannabis also known as AGLC hosts the "only regulated online gambling site in the province" known as Play Alberta (AGLC, n.d.). This is not the only regulated online gambling but rather Alberta was joining many other provinces across Canada that offer similar regulated platforms, dictated by each province (Mertz, 2020). Not only Play Alberta regulated but also the money generated through the website goes back into the "Government of Alberta's General Revenue Fund" and is used to support Alberta's social programs with an anticipated $3.71 million annual revenue (AGLC, n.d.; Mertz, 2020). Looking closer at the platform, there are multiple categories of games including "casino, instants, live dealer, lottery and game sense", in turn; these games attract a wide variety of people (PlayAlberta, n.d.). Although there are no concrete sources of revenue gained by playing these games online, one might compare it with casino statistics revealing that the payout of a slot machine is 92.4 percent of the money wagered, and the average general payout is between ninety and ninety-five percent depending on the game played (AGLC, 2012).

The last type of games that will be discussed are those that can be found on most mobile devices in the form of applications (apps). In a general search, many apps advertise the ability to pay the participant or user to use the app; however, only two will be used as an example. The first example of a get-paid-to app is Swagbucks, advertised by BuzzFeed, ABC and The Huffington Post, this app has users play games, answer surveys, watch videos, shop online and more (Boia et al., 2014; Swagbucks, 2021; Omololu, 2021). This service pays its users via PayPal or by redeemable gift cards for large retailers such as Amazon, Walmart and more (Rewards, 2021). To date, Swagbucks has paid its members $580,665,525 and estimates that "members who are light but regular daily users of the site can earn $500-$700 a year" (Swagbucks, 2021; Garrels, 2020). Another app that uses gameplay to reward players is Solitaire Cash; as a free app promising monetary rewards, it is ranked number two in the casino category of the Apple App Store and has a 4.7-star rating with 80.9 thousand reviews (Solitaire Cash, 2021). For free players, money comes through tournaments hosted in the game and through referrals, winning up to $7 from each tournament and an additional $1 for each player who joins with a personalized referral code (Ervin-Eickhoff, 2021). For those who are willing to spend some money with in-game purchases, some tournaments offer a $20 prize with a $7 entry fee (Ervin-Eickhoff, 2021). It has been concluded that apps are tailored more to the casual player rather than an individual who plays for high stakes or is deemed a professional.

Capitalizing on newly formed markets with the intention of making money is nothing new to society, it can be found in almost every aspect of human life. With the introduction of video games in the mid-1970s a new market for making money via online gaming was born. This has since grown into several different markets worth upwards of eight figures yearly, they include, Esports, streaming sites such as Twitch, online poker and casinos and finally smartphone applications. Arguably, the main reason for the explosion in popularity of making money via online games is down to the fact that every single adult has access to these types of markets due to the technological advancements made in the last fifty years.

# CHAPTER 5:

# WHAT NEWS AND SOCIAL MEDIA TELL US ABOUT VIDEO GAMES

**MAYA NAGORSKI**

# INTRODUCTION

From the point of their conception in 1958 (APS Physics, 2008), video games have astonished, compelled, and interacted with the public. Perceptions of these games have always been multifaceted, and have changed greatly over the years. On one hand, they became hugely popular in the 1980's, with culturally defining installments such as Donkey Kong, Tetris, and Legend of Zelda (Natural Museum of Play, 2016). On the other hand, they were often considered time wasters or negative influences on the youth (Greenfield, 2011). At this point in time, where does public opinion stand on video games? Is there still a concern that video games are linked to violence, or has research proven otherwise? Have video games responded to the recent demand for intersectional representation in media? Is the public coming to recognize cognitive or psychological benefits to playing video games? These questions, along with many others, contribute to the ever-changing perception of games and their role in our society.

# VIOLENCE IN VIDEO GAMES

One of the most widely spread critiques of video games is that they are liable to encourage violence in the impressionable youths that play them. This claim is supported by Bushman & Gibson (2010) who found that playing a violent video game for as little as 20 minutes could result in aggressive behaviour in men as much as 24 hours later, provided that the game was impactful enough to stay in the player's thoughts. This study concluded that since the violent content was appealing to the male subjects, it typically remained within their thoughts quite easily. Doğan (2006) posits that children who are routinely exposed to violence and aggression come to view it as the norm, mimicking the behaviour they watch and seeing no reason to put a stop to the mistreatment of others. Funk et al. (2003) conducted an experiment with 66 adolescents, and found that long-term exposure to such games is correlated with lower empathy. The impact of this has been well catalogued, with cases such Warren Leblanc's, wherein he stabbed his friend to death, supposedly influenced by the game 'Manhunt' (Doğan, 2006).

However, there are those that argue against this link between video games and violence. Haines (2005) conducted a study that found that exposure to the violent game 'Asheron's Call 2' had no significant effect on aggression in the subjects. Haines hypothesizes that this may be because of the fantastical nature of the game; perhaps games with unfamiliar surroundings are less dangerous than realistic games. Tom Kalinske, former president of SEGA, made a speech in 1994 where he asserted that children are able to tell the difference between real life and fiction, and moreover, that video games improve the social skills of children (Kalinske, 1994). Furthermore, Ferguson et al. (2009's) study found that a violent home environment is often a large factor in a child's behaviour. Once this factor was accounted for and controlled, they found that exposure to violent video games no longer correlated with violent acts. This study therefore posits that a player with a pre-existing violent personality will seek out violent content, but not that violent content creates the violent personality.

No matter the true extent to which video games promote violence, something that is still being researched and tested, the backlash and public concern around the topic has continued to grow. In response, a number of states in America have attempted to pass legislation to oversee the distribution of such games (Kenyota, 2008). None of these attempts has succeeded, due to concerns related to the First Amendment (Smith et al., 2006). Legislation in Australia allows the state to prohibit games that are unsuitable for children between the ages of 15 and 18, as determined by the Office of Film and Literature Classification (Rose-Steinberg, 2010). Likewise, the German government has the ability to ban games that seem to "describe...acts of violence against human beings in a manner which expresses a glorification or rendering harmless of such acts of violence..." specifically in response to violent crimes that appear to be motivated by aggressive games (Rose-Steinberg, 2010).

# BENEFITS

Notably, attention has begun to shift into how video games can benefit players and society. For example, teachers have begun examining how they might use video games as an educational resource (Schrader et al., 2006). As well as being a tool that students are willing to spend time with, video games can be used to develop problem-solving skills, active learning, and social behaviours. Furthermore, Koo & Seider (2010) argue that video games can be used to encourage an understanding of morals and ethics in youth, using the same logic that implies that violent video games lead to violent behaviour. They posit that the boundary between the fictional and real world can be crossed, and children will begin to mimic behaviours they see in the media they consume. As another benefit, Spence & Feng (2010) note that playing action games can have a significant effect on your cognition. Sensory and spatial awareness appear to improve, along with perception.

Beyond simply learning and development, video games may prove to be useful in other areas, such as rehabilitation and research. A study conducted into the effectiveness of using a Nintendo Wii Fit™ to treat balance impediments in patients with multiple sclerosis found that the exercise was enjoyable and challenging (Forsberg et al., 2015). Though the console was less effective in patients with Parkinson's disease, and caused some uncertainty in patients unfamiliar with the system, it is still a practical tool to encourage activity and treatment at home. Additionally, Karimpur & Hamburger (2015) have expressed the potential that video games have to improve psychological processes and human quality of life. With enough research and experimentation, video games could be used to develop rote-learning skills, increase gray matter in the brain, or treat disorders such as dyslexia or amblyopia. There is much to explore in terms of application of video games, though such work requires leaving behind the stigma surrounding gaming (Karimpur & Hamburger, 2015).

# REPRESENTATION

In recent years, public perception of video games has begun to center around representation of marginalized groups. 'Social identity reinforcement' can be incredibly important to certain individuals, specifically to those who feel they need their identity validated (Shaw, 2010). A study done by Rivadeneyra et al. (2007) found that not only the frequency of representation, but also the manner in which a child might see their community being portrayed has a significant impact on their concept of self; this study dealt with the effects of media representation on Latino children in the United States. They found that both the lack of representation and the perpetuation of cultural stereotypes led to negative body image and social self-esteem. A similar effect can be found in other marginalized audiences. Therefore, the public has begun to examine the video game industry's treatment of characters of different races, genders, or sexualities.

Traditionally, games have been designed to appeal to a largely male audience. Significant characters were rarely female, unless their purpose was to be sexualized (Ivory, 2006). Williams et al.'s survey in 2010 reaffirmed this, reporting a ratio of 85.23:14.77 of male characters to female characters. Gestos et al. (2018) went into depth investigating the effect this phenomenon has on the wellbeing of women. They found that women exposed to this kind of content reported feelings of low self-esteem and self-objectification. Furthermore, men exposed to this content were more likely to develop misogynistic views in everyday life. Finally, it would be a failure to discuss sexism in gaming without touching on GamerGate, a 2014 controversy surrounding the treatment of women in video games and game design. A group of men began to harass women online, feeling that women were ruining the world of gaming, forcing the inclusion of diverse characters and themes (Nieborg & Foxman, 2018). This continued to escalate until female game designers, such as Zoe Quinn, were threatened and even doxxed (Gray et al., 2016). As the movement gained traction, it forced the issue and gaming's history with sexism into the light. Creators and consumers alike were forced to consider how the ideals and messages long perpetuated by the industry allowed for the conception of such a movement.

In terms of race, video games are lacking in terms of proportional representation. Williams et al. (2010) found that in relation to the United States' demographic, Caucasian and Asian American individuals are over-represented while all other ethnicities are under-represented. With consideration to leading roles, all ethnicities other than Caucasian are under-represented. Beyond simply the appearance of diverse characters, how well does the video game industry portray different cultures? By Balela & Mundy (2015)'s rubric, this includes depictions of architecture, people, history, language, and more, as these are all integral parts of any given culture. This study examined 'Assassin's Creed 1' and 'Unearthed the Trail of Ibn Battuta'; two games greatly concerned with historical context, and still found that accuracy was often sacrificed for gameplay (Balela & Mundy, 2015). Other than oversimplifying or reducing foreign cultures, video games also have a historical problem with perpetuating racial stereotypes. Dill & Burgess (2012) conducted an experiment to prove how impactful this truly is in the everyday world, finding that players exposed to 'thug-like' black characters felt negatively towards black political candidates.


The LGBTQ+ community has gone underrepresented in video games for much of history. Any depictions of a queer person were often steeped in stereotypes and homophobia (Vitali, 2010). However, the number of queer characters has begun to rise over the years, specifically in the role play game (RPG) and adventure genres (Utsch et al., 2017). Nonbinary characters are still rare, but have seen an increase in frequency since 2002, with a similar trend being seen in transgender characters. Notably, the number of standalone games with queer characters doubled between 2013 and 2015 (Cole et al., 2017). However, one of the biggest obstacles the LGBTQ+ community has towards feeling represented is the ambiguity with which designers portray their characters. In response to this, Adrienne Shaw from Temple University created an online archive, titled The LGBTQ Video Game Archive, to record appearances of queer characters from the 1980's until the present, giving details as to how these characters have come to be perceived as queer (Mejeur, 2018). It is worth mentioning that LGBTQ+ representation varies greatly between different countries; as of 2017, France had not created any games with any explicitly queer characters, while Japan and America had produced 43 and 45 respectively (Utsch et al., 2017). As a means of escapism and expression, gaming has long been an important experience for the LGBTQ+ community. This is especially true in regards to transgender individuals, who are able to put themselves into the shoes of characters they truly identify with (Janiuk, 2014). For this reason, the increase in LGBTQ+ representation is worth celebration, though there are many steps yet to take.

# CULTURALLY IMPORTANT GAMES

Over the years, there have been games that create a lasting impact in the collective consciousness of society. An excellent example of this is Pokémon GO, a mobile gaming app that reached incredible heights of popularity in 2016. As an augmented reality game, Pokémon GO required players to walk around outdoors. On one hand, it encouraged physical exercise, a great boon to the video game industry, which has long been accused of contributing to the modern sedentary lifestyle (Kamboj & Krishna, 2017). Pokémon GO sparked a discussion as to how video games could be used to motivate healthier behaviours in the future. This was not limited to physical activity; Frith (2017) was inspired to examine how such games may even motivate behaviours such as voting. The use of augmented reality and "Pokéstops" proved to be beneficial to small businesses, as players would flock to these locations. A similar technique could feasibly be used to nudge players towards voting booths, charity drives, or donation centres (Frith, 2017). However, there was a public outcry about safety concerns, specifically in terms of players wandering around public spaces while being distracted by their screen (Needleman, 2016). Additionally, there were cases of criminals taking advantage of Pokéstops to attack unsuspecting players (Needleman, 2016). Another concern was that of privacy; as Pokémon GO is an augmented reality game, it depends on the player continuously providing information about their environment to the app (Harborth & Pape, 2017). In response, researchers such as Harborth & Pape (2019) began investigating the safety of such mobile apps. Pokémon GO's sudden surge in popularity led to many considering the mechanics, benefits, and potential problems in AR games.

Another example is Lara Croft, and the discussions around feminism that her games have sparked. An argument can certainly be made for Croft's empowerment; she is a female protagonist, conceived in a time where it was unusual for a woman to be anything other than a supporting character in a video game (Kennedy, 2002). This was a marvel in and of itself, and became the catalyst for more female-led games being developed in the future (Mikula, 2003). For another, Croft inhabited the traditionally masculine role of 'explorer', typically reserved for rugged heroes such as Indiana Jones; she never has to be 'saved' and instead performs daring feats of bravery (Kennedy, 2002). However, it cannot be ignored that Croft is extremely sexualized, both in form and costume design (Mikula, 2004). It has been said that Croft was created more to please the male audience than empower the female one. This has been a persistent dilemma for the video game industry and indeed the media industry as a whole; can the surge in female representation truly be considered a positive step forward if the female characters in question are one-dimensional and objectified? Lara Croft has become foundational to this discussion of what constitutes a true feminist role model.

## CONCLUSION

Public opinion surrounding video games has shifted significantly over time, as is to be expected for an industry so long lived. The negative impact that these games may have on our behaviours is still being investigated, along with the positive impact. Claims of increasing violence as well as claims of improving cognitive processes continue to coexist, with significant evidence from both sides. Moreover, society has come to look at gaming culture with a critical eye, scrutinizing its relationship with diversity and representation. As much as gaming seems to be evolving into something that can be enjoyed by anyone from any community, there are still hurdles to overcome and greater strides to take. Nonetheless, video games are unquestionably a large part of our culture, with different games continuously being brought into the spotlight and urging us to consider new questions about ourselves as a society.

# CHAPTER 6:

# WHY ARE VIDEO GAMES SO ADDICTIVE?

**BRIANNA BEDRAN**

# INTRODUCTION:

Video game addictions activates some similar brain regions associated with drug abuse such as the mesolimbic reward system and amygdala, and are similar in effect and pre-sensation to various behavioural addictions, such as gambling addictions (Matthews et al., 2019). Hence, to justify why video games are so addictive is often explained in research in association with other behavioural addiction. However, it is important to note that the theory of video game addictions being linked to other addictions is a rather outdated link and can lead to misperceptions, which is why in this chapter we will explore in depth feelings video game addictions can activate that lead to repetitive and constant use. A gaming disorder is defined by a cycle of persistent or recurrent gaming behavior. To be classified as a disorder, the behavioral pattern is severe enough to influence a significant involvement of family, social, educational, professional, or other relationships (Esposito et al., 2020). There is a general lack of agreement on the correct term used to define a gambling disorder. A variety of terms have been employed to describe this condition including: Excessive Internet addiction (encompassing gaming, social networking sites, and video viewing) or video game addiction; problematic computer game use, problematic video gaming, video game dependency, or pathological video gaming; or excessive gaming, pathological gaming, video game addiction, digital game addiction, or online gaming addiction (Esposito et al., 2020). The most conclusive data-however is still not exact; on video game addiction is the average player. Research suggests video games are especially popular among younger males, as 70% of young men and 90% of teenage boys play video games (Perrin, 2018). Moreover, the prototypic video game player is now 34 years old, plays video games for an average of eight hours a week, and has been playing for an average of 12 years" (Matthews et al., 2019). Although, anybody of any gender or age is drawn to video games and can develop a gaming disorder, and these statistics do not define the entire population of video game users.

# WHY VIDEO GAMES ARE SO ADDICTIVE?

The characteristics of video games may appeal to addictive behaviors. These characteristics respond to a "playful need," captivating people of all ages, sexes, and social classes (Mihara et al., 2017). The video game industry is rampant worldwide, with games running on mobile phones, computers, and video game devices. Video game use has even demonstrated some positive effects on basic mental processes such as perception, attention, memory, and decision-making (Eichenbaum et al., 2014). Nonetheless, abuse of this playful activity can become an addiction (Esposito et al., 2020). Parrott et al. explains that the key traits of a video game are rules, feedback, and self-presentation. Rules and guidelines explain what a player is permitted to do and what they cannot do in a game. Even when games are open world and promote autonomy while playing such as Grand Theft Auto 5, or allows players to build whatever they can imagine like in Minecraft, these independent games have limitations despite their degree of freedom. In the video game world, the more effective one is at mastering rules, the more skilled he or she is at that game. This skill level is communicated through the provided feedback while playing (Parrott et al., 2020). For example, in the video game Tom Clancy's Ghost Recon Wildlands, players complete a series of military missions. The game communicates with the player in a variety of ways to dictate their success or failure. Once in a mission, there may be several conditions for victory and another set of conditions for failure. In one mission, a player might need to interrogate a suspect. If the suspect is killed, the screen flashes, "mission failed." Conversely, if the mission is accomplished, the player earns experience points, wins new equipment, and progresses in the game's story (Parrott et al., 2020). This can be observed in many video games, and this feedback of failure or accomplishment tends to drive players more. If one fails, they will want to play over and over again until they get that flashing success screen. Once they have reached this success, this assures them they have mastered one level and drives them to master the next. The most prevalent aspect of video games that may contribute to addiction risk is this in-game reinforcement structure, which maintains continuous, interval, fixed, and/ or variable ratio reinforcement schedules. That may make some players more likely to engage in continued play (Matthews et al., 2019). These strategies may include incremental rewards such as leveling up a character; haphazard or fixed loot drops, which occur when a prize is provided after a player destroys an object or foe; winning/losing features such as dynamic difficulty adjustment (difficulty is adjusted as gamer plays); competitive leader boards that display players progress; and achievements, which include acknowledgement and rewards for successfully completing tasks. Research indicates that in-game reinforcement characteristics influence the video game's playability. Increases in positive reinforcement are associated with a higher likelihood of continuing or returning to play, and players find reward and punishment features to be some of the most enjoyable and important features in video games (Matthews et al., 2019)

The final trait is self-presentation. Players maintain a presence in the game, a representation of themselves in this virtual world; this could mean a character onscreen is serving as a more abstract, unseen entity that is involved in the digital game (Parrott et al., 2020). Research suggests that video games can provide feelings of intrinsic motivation, connections to characters, as well as positive emotions in their virtual reality. In turn, through feedback, rules, and self-presentation, a game can enhance positively valenced psychological outcomes for players. If a person is gratifying needs by playing video games while these needs are not being met elsewhere, such as in their life offline, it is not difficult to imagine how video game use might become problematic (Parrott et al., 2020). As we explained above, the rules of a game might compel one to fully master them, keeping the player playing. Another player might desire the feedback-rich environment of a game, because constantly receiving rewards and encouragement can be hooking, and create a sense of confidence. Further, players might perceive self-presentation in a game as a meaningful way to escape their daily routine and reality. Notably, heavy video game players may become desensitized to dopamine responses related to their game play. This could mean that players are compelled to play more in order to reach the once achieved satisfactory levels of dopamine. However, it is important to note that some commentators have argued that video game use is not this pathological (Parrott et al., 2020).

While research on the relationship between game genre and addiction is limited, studies suggest that massively multiplayer online role- playing games (MMORPGs) may be most strongly linked to problematic play. These games display a mixture of extensive reinforcement structures, opportunities for social interaction and competition, and never-ending game play. This combination of reinforcement features and self-presentation is often portrayed as particularly addicting and the highest levels of problematic play are reported among MMORPG gamers. Such reinforcing features may be associated with problematic play because they promote a state of flow, which occurs when a player experiences intense enjoyment from being immersed in the game, resulting in a distorted sense of time (Matthews et al., 2019)

Despite there being many sources to be found on video game disorders, there is a need for studies with greater heterogeneity to understand potentially addictive behavior, including that related to video games. In fact, there is a disagreement between some authors on the inclusion of the term disturbance of the game, stemming from the fact that gambling may not be the most appropriate starting point for considering behavioral addiction. However, there is still an open debate to identify addiction syndrome in comparison to behavioral dependence in a more specific way in order not to pathologies common behaviors. Furthermore, it is not yet explained how behaviors considered pathological can be related to the duration of the game, or how to understand the seriousness of dependent behaviors. This association is due to the fact that a gaming disorder shares many features with addictions related to psychoactive substances and with gambling disorder. The American Psychiatric Association applies to the behavior the same diagnostic criteria used for substance addictions, to new forms of behavioral addiction. Behavioral addictions—and therefore, those including video games—according to some experts, should be placed among "Impulse Behavior Disorders," as is already the case for gambling" (Esposito et al., 2020)

## IN-GAME PURCHASES

Another tactic to get players hooked on a video game is not necessarily the playing itself, but additional purchases to be made to improve their game time. In-game purchases ("microtransactions") are a common way for video game companies to continue to monetize their games long after the game has initially launched (Macphee, 2020). Captured by the anticipation, the flashing lights, and the triumphant sounds of the loot boxes, for players, the rewards that the loot boxes contain is not relevant; it is the act of opening them that invites them to buy more. This type of monetization system has influenced some gamers to develop addictive behavioral issues while spending copious amounts of money. The anticipation of uncertain rewards is linked to a dopamine release, which is responsible for motivating repeated behaviors (MacPhee, 2020) Video game companies make these loot box purchases a very simple process for gamers, encouraging them to spend more.

One may wonder how this industry's games being used by minors worldwide can get away with such corrupt tactics, but they succeed with their lack of government regulation. Video games are not subject to government regulation, and are rather self-regulated by the video game industry. There have been numerous governmental attempts to regulate video games and their content, but each attempt has been challenged by the Entertainment Software Association ("ESA") and subsequently struck down. The ESA has been highly successful in pushing back legislation on video games regulation, therefore any proposed legislation will likely be difficult to pass. Although there are many similarities between loot boxes and gambling, current gambling laws do not adequately regulate loot boxes (MacPhee, 2020)

MacPhee suggests to promote and continue the self-regulating success of the video game industry, the ESA should adopt two requirements that convey to customers the dangers of loot box systems in video games and limit their accessibility to children: (1) a warning prompt at the time of each loot box purchase that conveys information about the risks associated with such a system, and (2) a restriction on video game companies' ability to store credit card information for repeated loot box purchases, requiring gamers to input payment information for each purchase. These requirements would help to keep the video game industry self-regulating, as the United States will be less likely to pass legislation on loot boxes if regulations are already in place (Macphee, 2020).

## HIGH RISK GROUPS

Certain groups appear to be at higher risk for developing video game addiction than others, such as males, younger individuals (ages 16–21), and individuals with Attention-Deficit/Hyperactivity Disorder ADHD (Matthews et al., 2019) Altered reinforcement sensitivity may predispose individuals with ADHD to addictive, impulsive, and compulsive behaviors. Research suggests that people with ADHD experience reduced activity in cortical regions associated with attention, impulse control, and stimulus integration abilities, as well as heightened aware- ness of incoming stimuli (especially sight, sound, and touch), which may make them especially sensitive to the reinforcing stimuli in video games. This, along with deficits in focus, can provide difficulty for individuals with ADHD to manage their time and behaviors appropriately, potentially leading to difficulty managing video game play behaviors. Those with ADHD are also more susceptible to favour small immediate reinforcement over larger delayed reinforcement, meaning that they may be more strongly influenced by the reinforcement contingencies in video games than other individuals (Matthews et al., 2019).

## CONCLUSION

Though this chapter explores a rather dark side of video games, research and studies done on gaming disorders still lack a general agreement as to what defines a gaming addiction, and when/if it can become pathological. Thus, the information presented here is certainly not conclusive. Moreover, as described in chapter four of this book there are some pros to gaming, and this chapter does not suggest that video games are all bad and prey on individuals. If you or somebody you know notices it influencing day to day life and relationships, perhaps then this behaviour will invoke some concern. Nevertheless, similar to other addictions there are always ways to seek help from family, friends, and/or therapy.

# REFERENCES:

Parenting Science. (2021). Video games and attention: gaming inhances some skills and hinders others. https://parentingscience.com/video-games-and-attention.

GamesBeat. (Apr 16, 2013). Why do we love video games? https://venturebeat.com/community/2013/04/16/why-do-we-love-video-games.

Teachthought. (n.d). Why People Play Video Games. https://www.teachthought.com/learning/why-people-play-video-games.

Lifehack. (2021). 10 Reasons Why Adults Who Play Video Games Are Happier. https://www.lifehack.org/articles/lifestyle/10-reasons-why-adults-who-play-video-games-are-happier.

The Sydney Morning Herald. (Dec 17, 2018). Why Do Men And Boys Crave Their Video Games. https://amp.smh.com.au/national/why-men-and-boys-crave-their-video-games.

Frontiers in Psychology. (Jul 26, 2019). The Association Between Video Gaming And Psychological Functioning. https://www.frontiersin.org/articles.

Medical News Today. (Jul 10, 2017). How Video Games Affect The Brain. https://www.medicalnewstoday.com/articles/324170#_noHeaderPrefixedContent.

UK Rehab. (nd). Gaming Addiction, How Gaming Affects The Brain. https://www.uk-rehab.com/behavioral-addictions/gaming.

Adžić, S., Al-Mansour, J., Naqvi, H., & Stambolić, S. (2021). The impact of video games on Students' educational outcomes. Entertainment Computing, 38, 100412.

https://doi.org/10.1016/j.entcom.2021.100412

Anderson, C., & Murphy, C. (2003). Violent Video Games and Aggressive Behavior in Young

Women. Aggressive Behavior, 29, 423–429. https://doi.org/10.1002/ab.10042

Annetta, L. A. (2008). Video Games in Education: Why They Should Be Used and How They

Are Being Used. Theory Into Practice, 47(3), 229–239.

https://doi.org/10.1080/00405840802153940

Burnay, J. (n.d.). Sexualization and aggression against women: A focus on sexualized characters

in video games. 287.

Cain, N., & Gradisar, M. (2010). Electronic media use and sleep in school-aged children and

adolescents: A review. Sleep Medicine, 11(8), 735–742.

https://doi.org/10.1016/j.sleep.2010.02.006

Gentile, D. A., Lynch, P. J., Linder, J. R., & Walsh, D. A. (2004). The effects of violent video

game habits on adolescent hostility, aggressive behaviors, and school performance.

Journal of Adolescence, 27(1), 5–22. https://doi.org/10.1016/j.adolescence.2003.10.002

Gupta, A., Lawendy, B., Goldenberg, M. G., Grober, E., Lee, J. Y., & Perlis, N. (2021). Can video games enhance surgical skills acquisition for medical students? A systematic review. Surgery, 169(4), 821–829. https://doi.org/10.1016/j.surg.2020.11.034

King, D. L., Gradisar, M., Drummond, A., Lovato, N., Wessel, J., Micic,

G., Douglas, P., & Delfabbro, P. (2013). The impact of prolonged violent video-gaming on adolescent sleep:

An experimental study. Journal of Sleep Research, 22(2), 137–143.

https://doi.org/10.1111/j.1365-2869.2012.01060.x

Reynaldo, C., Christian, R., Hosea, H., & Gunawan, A. A. S. (2021). Using Video Games to

Improve Capabilities in Decision Making and Cognitive Skill: A Literature Review.

Procedia Computer Science, 179, 211–221. https://doi.org/10.1016/j.procs.2020.12.027

Selvakumarasamy, S., Joseph James, S., Arun, C., & Karthick, S. (2021). Basic education for

autistic children using interactive video games. Materials Today: Proceedings.

https://doi.org/10.1016/j.matpr.2021.01.455

Swing, E. L., Gentile, D. A., Anderson, C. A., & Walsh, D. A. (2010). Television and Video

Game Exposure and the Development of Attention Problems. Pediatrics, 126(2),

214–221. https://doi.org/10.1542/peds.2009-1508

Weigle, P. E. (2017). 81.2 Prescribing Playstation: When Video Games Are Good for Kids.

Journal of the American Academy of Child & Adolescent Psychiatry, 56(10,

Supplement), S120. https://doi.org/10.1016/j.jaac.2017.07.472

AGLC. (2012). Player Information: A Guide to Gambling Responsibly [Brochure]. https://reelfacts.aglc.ca/siteuploads/document/aglc_brochure_april2013.pdf

AGLC. (n.d.). What is Play Alberta?. https://aglc.ca/playalberta

Bányai, F., Griffiths, M., Király, O., & Demetrovics, Z. (2019). The psychology of esports: A systematic literature review. Journal of Gambling Studies, 35, 351-365. http://irep.ntu.ac.uk/id/eprint/32858/1/PubSub10417_Griffiths.pdf

Boia, M., Musat, C.C., & Faltings, B. (2014). Constructing Context-Aware Sentiment Lexicons with an Asynchronous Game with a Purpose. In A. Gelbukh (Eds.), Computational Linguistics and Intelligent Text Processing (pp. 32-44). Springer, Heidelberg. https://doi.org/10.1007/978-3-642-54903-8_3

Ervin-Eickhoff, B. (2021, March 2). Solitaire Cash Review-Win Real Money Playing Solitaire Against Others Online. Joywallet. https://joywallet.com/solitaire-cash-review/

Europe's Largest Mid-Stakes Series has Returned. (2021). GGPoker. https://en.ggpoker.com/tournaments/battle-of-malta-online-series-2021/

Gainsbury, S. (2015). Online Gambling Addiction: the Relationship Between Internet Gambling and Disordered Gambling. Current addiction reports, 2(2), 185-193. https://doi.org/10.1007/s40429-015-0057-8

Garrels, S. (2020, July 16). Max Out Your Swagbucks Account - How to Earn Even More!. Swagbucks. https://www.swagbucks.com/articles/max-out-your-swagbucks-account

Geyser, W. (2021, June 21). How Much do YouTubers Make?- A YouTuber's Pocket Guide [Calculator]. Influencer Marketing Hub. https://influencermarketinghub.com/how-much-do-youtubers-make/#:~:text=How%20much%20does%20a%20YouTuber,%245%20per%201000%20video%20views.

Griffiths, M.D. (2005). Online betting exchanges: A brief overview. Youth Gambling International, 5(2), 1-2.

Griffiths, M.D., Parke, A., Wood, R.T.A., & Parke, J. (2006). Internet gambling: An overview of psychosocial impacts. Gaming Research and Review Journal, 27(1), 27-39. https://digitalscholarship.unlv.edu/cgi/viewcontent.cgi?article=1149&context=grrj

Hamari, J. & Sjöblom, M. (2017). What is eSports and why do people watch it?. Internet Research, 27(2), 1-34. https://trepo.tuni.fi/bitstream/handle/10024/101034/what_is_esports_and_2017.pdf?sequence=1&isAllowed=y

Himmelstein, D., Liu, Y., & Shapiro, J. L. (2017). An exploration of mental skills among competitive League of Legend players. International Journal of Gaming and Computer-Mediated Simulations, 9(2), 1-21.

How to earn money on YouTube. (2021). YouTube Help. https://support.google.com/youtube/answer/72857?hl=en

Kresse, C. (2016, January 8). eSports in 2015 by the numbers: Attendance figures, investments and prize money, Esports Marketing Blog

Mangeloja, E. (2019). Economics of Esports. Electronic Journal of Business Ethics and Organization Studies, 24(2), 34-42. https://jyx.jyu.fi/bitstream/handle/123456789/66616/ejbo_vol24_no2_pages_34-42.pdf?sequence=1

Marinkovic, P. (2020, July 2020). Esports Pro Gamers: How Much Do They Earn?. Superjump. https://superjumpmagazine.com/esports-pro-gamers-how-much-do-they-earn-f03a1d047190

Martz, E. (2020, October 1). PlayAlberta, regulated online gambling website, launched Thursday. Global News. https://globalnews.ca/news/7371803/playalberta-regulated-online-gambling-website/

Omololu, E. (2021, May 9). 25 Free Money Making Apps That Pay Cash in 2021. Savvy New Canadians. https://www.savvynewcanadians.com/best-money-making-apps/

Partners. (2021). Cloud9. https://cloud9.gg/partners/

Pitt, M. & Glatzer, J. (2021, July 26). High Stakes Action Explodes at GGPoker; Battle of Malta Champion Crowned. Pokernews. https://www.pokernews.com/news/2021/07/high-stakes-action-explodes-at-ggpoker-39546.htm

PlayAlberta. (n.d.). https://playalberta.ca/

Rewards. (2021). Swagbucks. https://www.swagbucks.com/rewards-store

Rosen, S. (1981). The economics of superstars. The American Economic Review, 71(5), 845–858. https://www.jstor.org/stable/1803469?origin=JSTOR-pdf

Shillibier, W. (2021, July 7). $25M GTD Battler of Malta Online Festival Returns to GGPoker this July. Pokernews. https://www.pokernews.com/news/2021/07/battle-of-malta-online-festival-returns-to-ggpoker-39452.htm

Solitaire Cash. (2021). Apple. https://apps.apple.com/us/app/solitaire-cash/id1446254576

Swagbucks. (2021). https://www.swagbucks.com/

Taylor, N. (2016). Play to the camera: Video ethnography, spectatorship, and e-sports. Convergence, 22(2), 115-130. https://doi.org/10.1177/1354856515580282

Twitch Turbo. (n.d.). Twitch. https://www.twitch.tv/turbo

Twitch Affiliate Partner Program. (n.d.). Business of Apps. https://www.businessofapps.com/affiliate/twitch/

Ward, M., & Harmon, A. (2019). Esport Superstars. Journal of Economics, 1(27), 1-27. DOI: 10.1177/1527002519859417

Wood, R.T.A., & Griffiths, M.D. (2008) Why Swedish people play online poker and factors that can increase or decrease trust in poker Web sites: A qualitative investigation. Journal of Gambling, 21(7), 80-97. http://irep.ntu.ac.uk/id/eprint/22650/1/200183_6573%20Griffiths%20Publisher.pdf

Wood, R.T.A., Parke, J., & Griffiths, M.D. (2007). The acquisition, development, and maintenance of online poker playing in a student sample. CyberPsychology and Behavior, 10(3), 354-361. http://doi.org/10.1089/cpb.2006.9944

APS Physics. (2008, October). October 1958: Physicist Invents first video game. American Physical Society. https://www.aps.org/publications/apsnews/200810/physicshistory.cfm.

Balela, M. S., & Mundy, D. (2015). Analysing Cultural Heritage and its Representation in Video Games. In DiGRA Conference.

Bushman, B. J., & Gibson, B. (2011). Violent video games cause an increase in aggression long after the game has been turned off. Social Psychological and Personality Science, 2(1), 29-32.

Cole, A., Shaw, A., & Zammit, J. (2017). Representations of queer identity in games from 2013–2015. Extended Abstract Presented at DiGRA.

Dill, K. E., & Burgess, M. C. (2013). Influence of black masculinity game exemplars on social judgments. Simulation & Gaming, 44(4), 562-585.

Doğan, F. Ö. (2006). Video games and children: violence in video games. In New/Yeni Symposium Journal (Vol. 44, No. 4, pp. 161-164).

Ferguson, C. J., Rueda, S. M., Cruz, A. M., Ferguson, D. E., Fritz, S., & Smith, S. M. (2008). Violent video games and aggression: Causal relationship or byproduct of family violence and intrinsic violence motivation?. Criminal Justice and Behavior, 35(3), 311-332.

Forsberg, A., Nilsagård, Y., & Boström, K. (2015). Perceptions of using videogames in rehabilitation: a dual perspective of people with multiple sclerosis and physiotherapists. Disability and rehabilitation, 37(4), 338-344.

Frith, J. (2017). The digital "lure": Small businesses and Pokémon Go. Mobile Media & Communication, 5(1), 51-54.

Funk, J. B., Buchman, D. D., Jenks, J., & Bechtoldt, H. (2003). Playing violent video games, desensitization, and moral evaluation in children. Journal of Applied Developmental Psychology, 24(4), 413-436.

Gestos, M., Smith-Merry, J., & Campbell, A. (2018). Representation of women in video games: a systematic review of literature in consideration of adult female wellbeing. Cyberpsychology, Behavior, and Social networking, 21(9), 535-541.

Gray, K. L., Buyukozturk, B., & Hill, Z. G. (2017). Blurring the boundaries: Using Gamergate to examine "real" and symbolic violence against women in contemporary gaming culture. Sociology Compass, 11(3), e12458.

Greenfield, P. M. (2011). Video games revisited. In Gaming and Simulations: Concepts, Methodologies, Tools and Applications (pp. 306-325). IGI Global.

Harborth, D., & Pape, S. (2017, September). Privacy concerns and behavior of Pokémon go players in Germany. In IFIP International Summer School on Privacy and Identity Management (pp. 314-329). Springer, Cham.

Harborth, D., & Pape, S. (2019, December). Investigating Privacy Concerns Related to Mobile Augmented Reality Applications. In ICIS.

Ivory, J. D. (2006). Still a man's game: Gender representation in online reviews of video games. Mass Communication & Society, 9(1), 103-114.

Janiuk, J. (2014, March 5). Gaming is my safe space: Gender options are important for the transgender community. Polygon. https://www.polygon.com/2014/3/5/5462578/gaming-is-my-safe-space-gender-options-are-important-for-the.

Kalinske, T. (2014, August 18) Video Games Do Not Cause Aggressive Behavior in Children [Paper presentation]. Commonwealth Club of California, San Francisco, California, United States.

Kamboj, A. K., & Krishna, S. G. (2017). Pokémon GO: An innovative smartphone gaming application with health benefits. Primary care diabetes, 11(4), 397-399.

Karimpur, H., & Hamburger, K. (2015). The future of action video games in psychological research and application. Frontiers in psychology, 6, 1747.

Kennedy, H. W. (2002). Lara Croft: Feminist icon or cyberbimbo?. Game studies, 2(2), 1-12.

Kenyota, G. (2007). Thinking of the children: The failure of violent video game laws. Fordham Intell. Prop. Media & Ent. LJ, 18, 785.

Koo, G., & Seider, S. (2010). Video games for prosocial learning. In Ethics and game design: Teaching values through play (pp. 16-33). IGI Global.

Mejeur, C. J. (2018). Preserving and Visualizing Queer Representation in Video Games. Digital Humanities 2018: Book of Abstracts/Libro de resúmenes.

Mikula, M. (2003). Gender and Videogames: the political valency of Lara Croft. Continuum, 17(1), 79-87.

Mikula, M. (2004). Lara Croft: Between a feminist icon and male fantasy. Femme Fatalities. Representations of Strong Women in the Media, eds. R. Schubart and A. Gjelsik, 57-70.

Natural Museum of Play. (2016, March 24). Video game history timeline. Video Game History Timeline | The Strong. https://www.museumofplay. org/about/icheg/video-game-history/timeline.

Needleman, S. E. (2016). 'Pokémon Go'Craze Raises Safety Issues. Wall Street Journal.

Nieborg, D., & Foxman, M. (2018). Mainstreaming misogyny: The beginning of the end and the end of the beginning in gamergate coverage. In Mediating misogyny (pp. 111-130). Palgrave Macmillan, Cham.

Rivadeneyra, R., Ward, L. M., & Gordon, M. (2007). Distorted reflections: Media exposure and Latino adolescents' conceptions of self. Media Psychology, 9(2), 261-290.

Rose-Steinberg, J. (2010). Gaming the system: An examination of the constitutionality of violent video game legislation. Seton Hall Legis. J., 35, 198.

Schrader, P. G., Zheng, D., & Young, M. (2006). Teachers' perceptions of video games: MMOGs and the future of preservice teacher education. Innovate: Journal of Online Education, 2(3).

Shaw, A. (2010). Identity, identification, and media representation in video game play: An audience reception study (Doctoral dissertation, University of Pennsylvania).

Smith, P. M., Fallow, K. A., Pozza, D. C., & Hellman, M. S. (2006). Attack on Violent Video Games. Comm. Law., 24, 1.

Spence, I., & Feng, J. (2010). Video games and spatial cognition. Review of General Psychology, 14(2), 92-104.

Utsch, S., Bragança, L. C., Ramos, P., Caldeira, P., & Tenorio, J. (2017). Queer Identities in Video Games: Data visualization for a quantitative analysis of representation. Proceedings of SBGames, 850-851.

Vitali, D. M. (2010). From bullies to heroes: Homophobia in video games. Inquiries Journal, 2(02).

Williams, D., Martins, N., Consalvo, M., & Ivory, J. D. (2009). The virtual census: Representations of gender, race and age in video games. New media & society, 11(5), 815-834.

Eichenbaum, A.; Bavelier, D.; Green, C.S. (2014). Video games: Play that can do serious good. Am. J. Play, 7, 50–72.

Esposito, M. R., Serra, N., Guillari, A., Simeone, S., Sarracino, F., Continisio, G. I., & Rea, T. (2020). An investigation into video game addiction in pre-adolescents and adolescents: A cross-sectional study. Medicina, 56(5), 221. https://doi.org/10.3390/medicina56050221

MacPhee, M. J. (2020). new form of addiction: practical regulatory approach towards randomized reward systems in video games to protect consumers from gambling-like practices. Washburn Law Journal, 59(1), 137-170.

Mathews, C. L., Morrell, H. E., & Molle, J. E. (2018). Video game addiction, adhd symptomatology, and video game reinforcement. The American Journal of Drug and Alcohol Abuse, 45(1), 67–76. https://doi.org/10.1080/00952990.2018.1472269

Mihara, S.; Higuchi, S. (2017) Cross-sectional and longitudinal epidemiological studies of Internet gaming disorder: A systematic review of the literature. Psychiatry Clin. Neuroscis, 71, 425–444.

Parrott, S., Rogers, R., Towery, N. A., & Hakim, S. D. (2020). Gaming disorder: News media framing of video game addiction as a mental illness. Journal of Broadcasting & Electronic Media, 64(5), 815–835. https://doi.org/10.1080/08838151.2020.1844887

Perrin, A. (2018). 5 facts about Americans and video games. Pew Research Center. https://www.pewresearch.org/fact-tank/2018/09/17/5-facts-about- americans-and-video-games/